BIBLICAL WOMEN

ALSO BY JOHN F. FINK

Published by ST PAULS:

Married Saints

The Doctors of the Church: Doctors of the First Millennium

The Doctors of the Church: Doctors of the Second Millennium

American Saints

Letters to St. Francis de Sales: Mostly on Prayer

Jesus in the Gospels

By Other Publishers:

Moments in Catholic History

Travels With Jesus in the Holy Land

Patriotic Leaders of the Church

Memoirs of a Catholic Journalist

The Mission and Future of the Catholic Press (Editor)

Biblical Women

Females in a Patriarchal Society

JOHN F. FINK

ST PAULS

Library of Congress Cataloging-in-Publication Data

Fink, John F.
Biblical women : females in a patriarchal society / by John F. Fink.
p. cm.
ISBN-13: 978-0-8189-1262-7
ISBN-10: 0-8189-1262-6
1. Women in the Bible. 2. Bible—Biography. I. Title.
BS575.F57 2008
220.9'2082—dc22
2007048680

Produced and designed in the United States of America by the Fathers and Brothers of the Society of St. Paul,
2187 Victory Boulevard, Staten Island, New York 10314-6603
as part of their communications apostolate.

ISBN 10: 0-8189-1262-6
ISBN 13: 978-0-8189-1262-7

Printing Information:

Current Printing - first digit 1 2 3 4 5 6 7 8 9 10

Year of Current Printing - first year shown

2008 2009 2010 2011 2012 2013 2014 2015

For Marie,
our three daughters
and six granddaughters

TABLE OF CONTENTS

Introduction ix

Part I
WOMEN IN THE OLD TESTAMENT

1. Did Eve have a belly button? 3
2. Lot's Wife and Daughters 5
3. The First Surrogate Mother 8
4. A Mother with a Favorite Son 11
5. Jacob's Wives and Consorts 14
6. The Story of Judah and Tamar 17
7. The Story of Potiphar's Wife 20
8. Miriam and Zipporah 23
9. Rahab Saves Joshua's Spies 26
10. The Story of Deborah and Jael 29
11. Jephthah Kills His Daughter 32
12. The Mother of Samson 35
13. Samson's Philistine Wife 38
14. Delilah Betrays Samson 41
15. The Story of Ruth and Naomi 44
16. Peninnah and Hannah 47
17. David's First Wife, Michal 50

18. David's Third Wife, Abigail 53
19. The Beautiful Bathsheba 56
20. The Rape of Tamar 59
21. The Queen of Sheba 62
22. Jezebel, Ahab's Wicked Wife 65
23. Athaliah and Jehosheba 68
24. The Story of Sarah and Tobiah 71
25. Judith Defeats Holofernes 74
26. Esther Saves the Jews 77
27. Mother and Sons Are Martyred 80

Part II
WOMEN IN THE NEW TESTAMENT

28. Elizabeth, Wife of Zechariah 85
29. Mary, the Mother of God 88
30. The Woman at the Well 95
31. Herodias and Salome 98
32. Stories of Two Public Sinners 101
33. Mary Magdalene 104
34. Martha and Mary of Bethany 107
35. Four Whom Jesus Healed 110
36. Witnesses to the Crucifixion 113
37. Sapphira, Tabitha and Lydia 116
38. Mark's Mother and Rhoda 119
39. Prisca, Paul's Collaborator 122

INTRODUCTION

Who can deny that the Bible describes a patriarchal society? Can you imagine the size of a book called *Biblical Men*? The world from the time of creation through the time that Jesus lived on earth was controlled by men. There's just no way to get around the fact that women played a subservient role.

Nevertheless, women in the Bible also played an important role, if sometimes only as the mothers of those dominant men. Occasionally they are known *only* as the mothers of those men—like Samson's mother for example. Apparently her name wasn't important enough for the author to record.

On the other hand, several of the women managed to secure important positions in the Israelites' society. An example is Deborah, who became one of the Israelites' judges and commanded the army to fight. Some women did heroic deeds even if they weren't actually in positions of authority—Judith, for example, or Esther.

In this short book I've told the stories of 39 of the most prominent women in the Bible. Some of them are heroes such as those mentioned. Others, such as Jezebel and Herodias, are villains. Some are saints, most notably, of course, Mary the mother of God. Others, such as the woman who washed Jesus' feet with her tears, and the woman caught in adultery, are sinners.

Perhaps no stories illustrate the patriarchal society of the Old Testament better than those of Jephthah's daughter and the rape of Tamar. The three chapters about three of King David's wives, or the stories about Jacob's wives and consorts, exemplify the polygamy that existed among the Israelites of that era. However, other stories show how the women were able to get their way in a patriarchal society—Rebekah, for example, or Abigail.

There are touching stories such as the relationship between Naomi and Ruth, or between Jesus and Mary of Bethany. But the women could also be ruthless at times as, for example, Jael and Judith.

In this book, I won't get into discussions about whether or not some of the women, especially those in Genesis, actually existed. I will tell their stories just as the Bible does.

I can't cover all of the women in the Bible, but just the main characters. They're interesting and intriguing. I hope my stories of these women will encourage you to read about them yourself.

This obviously is a small book in size. There are two reasons for that. First it's simply because we don't know much more about these women. Secondly, though, it's because I want to use the chapters in this book as columns in *The Criterion*, the newspaper of the Archdiocese of Indianapolis.

I hope you will enjoy and profit from learning about these biblical women.

John F. Fink

PART I

WOMEN IN THE OLD TESTAMENT

1

DID EVE HAVE A BELLY BUTTON?

The logical place to start is with Eve. It's been said that she is the only woman who didn't have a belly button since she was never a fetus. According to the second chapter of the Book of Genesis, "God built up into a woman the rib that he had taken from the man." He then took her to Adam as a mature woman.

What does this story do to the theory of evolution? The Bible is not a scientific text, especially the first eleven chapters of Genesis. As *The Catholic Study Bible* says, "As literature, Genesis 1-11 is defined as 'myth,' in which every story seems to describe some sort of model, for bad or for good, of the proper relations of God to the world of humans."

And what do we learn from the story of Adam and Eve? First of all, we learn that man and woman are meant to complement and complete one another. Genesis says of all the animals, "None proved to be the suitable partner for man." Not so the woman. She is, Adam says, "bone of my bones and flesh of my flesh," and the narrative says, "That is why a man leaves his father and mother and clings to his wife, and the two of them become one body." Conjugal union is willed by God.

But, unfortunately, Adam and Eve didn't live happily ever after. Chapter 3 tells us of their fall after a serpent tempted Eve to disobey God's order not to eat of the fruit of the "tree of knowledge of good and evil." She ate the fruit and then gave some to Adam, who also ate it. The immediate result was that they realized for the first time that they were naked, felt shame for that fact and made loincloths to cover their nakedness.

When God came to see what had happened, they hid from him, but to no avail. In punishment for their disobedience, they were expelled from the Garden of Eden. Their happy times were over. Because of her disobedience, sin and death came into the world—not only for them but for the entire human race. From then on Adam and Eve had to work for their living and experience hardships. Eve was told, "I will intensify the pangs of your childbearing; in pain shall you bring forth children. Yet your urge shall be for your husband, and he shall be your master."

She did bring forth children, of course—Cain, Abel and Seth, at least, for they are mentioned by name. Chapter 5 says that Adam had other sons and daughters but they aren't mentioned by name and they would not necessarily have been Eve's children. She also had to bear the anguish of learning that her son Cain murdered her son Abel.

2

LOT'S WIFE AND DAUGHTERS

Lot was Abraham's nephew. The two of them migrated together from Ur, in southern Mesopotamia, to the land of Canaan. Then they separated and Lot pitched his tents near Sodom. He and his wife and daughters were the only good people in Sodom or the neighboring town of Gomorrah. When God became determined to destroy Sodom and Gomorrah because of their wickedness, he sent two angels, disguised as humans, to rescue Lot and his family.

Genesis 19 shows us how evil the residents of Sodom were. When they learned that two strangers were staying with Lot, they surrounded Lot's house (he apparently was no longer living in a tent). They demanded that Lot "bring them out to us that we may have intimacies with them."

Lot tried to placate the men in a way that we can only consider shocking, and also clearly demonstrates the subsidiary role of women in that society. He offered to give them his two virgin daughters rather than let them violate the men to whom he had given hospitality. This didn't placate the Sodomites, who tried to break down the door to the house. But the angels struck the men outside with a blinding light.

The angels then led Lot and his wife and daughters out of Sodom, into the hills, as God began to destroy the city with fire. They told them not to look back or stop. "But Lot's wife looked back, and she was turned into a pillar of salt" (Genesis 19:26).

Lot's wife appears in the Book of Wisdom as "the tomb of a disbelieving soul, a standing pillar of salt" (Wisdom 10:7), and Jesus said, "Remember the wife of Lot" when telling people that, on the coming of the Kingdom of God, a person in the field must not return to what was left behind (Luke 17:32).

Lot and his two daughters were now safe, living in a cave. But it was a lonely existence for two young women. They had both been engaged and Lot had tried to get their fiancés to leave Sodom with them, but the men didn't believe him when he said that God was going to destroy the town.

Deprived of men their age, and wanting to have children, the two women decided to take matters into their own hands. Lot was the only man around. So they plied their father with wine until he fell asleep and then the older of his daughters slept with him. They did the same thing the next night, this time the younger daughter taking her turn.

Somehow, they managed to do this without Lot's knowledge even though he was able to perform.

Both women became pregnant. The older daughter gave birth to a boy they named Moab, who became the ancestor of the Moabites. The younger daughter gave birth to a boy they named Ammon, the ancestor of the Ammonites.

This Israelite story about the incestuous birth of Moab and Ammon was obviously included in their Scriptures to ridicule the Moabites and Ammonites, Israel's rival nations on the east side of the Jordan River and the Dead Sea.

3

THE FIRST SURROGATE MOTHER

Abram's wife Sarai was a beautiful woman. Twice Abram passed her off as his sister because he was afraid that men they met during their nomadic life would kill him in order to get Sarai.

The first time (Genesis 12:10-20) was when they went to Egypt because of a famine in Canaan. That time the Pharaoh took Sarai as his wife and gave flocks and herds to Abram. When he learned that Abram had deceived him, he returned Sarai to Abram and told him to leave Egypt.

The same thing happened later (Genesis 20: 1-18) after God changed their names to Abraham and Sarah. This time they were living in the Negeb when Abimelech, king of Gerar, took Sarah as his wife after Abraham told him that she was his sister. But before Abimelech could "approach" Sarah, God appeared to him in a dream and told him that Sarah was Abraham's wife. He, too, restored her to him and he, too, gave flocks and herds, and even male and female slaves, to Abraham.

Throughout all this time, Sarai had been unable to have children. God had promised Abram that he would be the father of many nations, but how was this to happen if Sarai remained barren? It was Sarai who came up with a solution (Genesis 16:1-16): "Have intercourse with my maid [Hagar]; perhaps I shall have sons through her," she said to Abram. He did, and Hagar became history's first surrogate mother.

Then, though, as sometimes happens in cases like this, Hagar's attitude toward Sarai changed: "She looked on her mistress with disdain." In turn, Sarai abused Hagar so much that she ran away. But God in human form found Hagar in the wilderness and sent her back to Sarai.

Hagar bore Ishmael, who would become the father of the Arab nations. When Ishmael was thirteen, God made his covenant with Abram and his descendants. God demanded that all males be circumcised as a mark of the covenant. This was also when he changed Abram's and Sarai's names.

God, though, still promised that Sarah would have a child, though she was now ninety. Once three visitors (one of whom was God) arrived and told Abraham that Sarah would have a son, which made Sarah laugh to herself. God asked why Sarah laughed and she denied laughing. But God said, "Yes you did."

Sarah did indeed bear a son, whom they called Isaac. Now that she had her own son, Sarah became even more hostile toward Hagar and Ishmael, demanding that Abraham send them away.

Abraham did so, and once again God found Hagar, this time with Ishmael, roaming aimlessly in the wilderness. He promised Hagar that Ishmael would be the father of a great nation. Ishmael grew up and became an expert bowman. Hagar got a wife for him in Egypt. They had twelve sons.

Sarah died at age one hundred twenty-seven in Hebron, where Abraham buried her. She was the first of Israel's patriarchs and matriarchs to be buried there.

4

A MOTHER WITH A FAVORITE SON

"Mom likes you best."

That's a Tommy Smothers' line, but Esau could have said it to Jacob.

In this case, "Mom" was Rebekah, Isaac's wife. She had been born in Mesopotamia. As Abraham was dying in Canaan, he commanded his servant to return to Abraham's original homeland in Mesopotamia to find a wife for Isaac because he didn't want him to marry a Canaanite. Rebekah was the daughter of Bethuel and the sister of Laban.

The servant prayed to God to point out the right wife for Isaac. He prayed that, when he asked a woman by a spring for some water, she would not only give him a drink but would also draw water for his camels. That would be a sign that she was to be Isaac's wife. When Rebekah approached the spring, she did exactly that.

After the servant explained his mission, Rebekah took him to meet her family. The servant presented objects of gold and silver and clothing to Rebekah as well as to Laban and Rebekah's mother. That seems to have been all it took to get Rebekah to agree to go with the servant and to become Isaac's wife.

Isaac married Rebekah when he was forty. They had no children for twenty years, but then Rebekah became pregnant with twins: Esau, with reddish skin and a hairy body; and Jacob, with smooth skin. As they grew up, Isaac preferred Esau, but Rebekah liked Jacob more.

Eventually Isaac grew elderly and blind. Thinking that he was about to die, he wanted to give a special blessing to Esau. He told Esau to hunt some game and to prepare an appetizing dish for him before he gave him his blessing.

Rebekah overheard this. She was a conniver and determined to get that blessing for Jacob. So she prepared an appetizing dish for Isaac. She dressed Jacob in Esau's clothing and covered his hands and neck with skins from the kids they killed to make the dinner.

The ruse worked. Although Isaac was suspicious because the voice he heard sounded like Jacob, he felt the hairy hands and neck and smelled Esau's clothing. He ate the meal that Jacob had brought and gave him his special blessing.

No sooner had Jacob left his father than Esau arrived. When they both understood what had happened, Isaac insisted that he had only one blessing to give and he had given it to Jacob. Now, he said, Esau would have to serve his brother Jacob.

Naturally, Esau was furious. He vowed to kill Jacob. Rebekah realized what Esau had in mind, so she told Jacob to flee to her brother Laban in Mesopotamia. To Isaac she explained why Jacob was going to Laban by saying that she didn't want him to marry a Canaanite woman. Esau had already married a Hittite woman named Judith and a Hivite woman named Basemath.

Rebekah paid for her deception. She would not live to see Jacob again. But Isaac did, living much longer than expected.

5

JACOB'S WIVES AND CONSORTS

In the previous chapter I wrote about the way Rebekah and her son Jacob deceived Isaac, Rebekah's husband and Jacob's father. This week it's Jacob's turn to be deceived.

Jacob returned to Mesopotamia to escape Esau's wrath and to find a wife. He no sooner reached Haran, where Rebekah had grown up, than he met Rachel, the younger daughter of his uncle Laban, Rebekah's brother. Laban also had an older daughter, Leah.

The Bible says, "Leah had lovely eyes, but Rachel was well formed and beautiful" (Genesis 29: 17). Jacob immediately fell in love with Rachel. He proposed to Laban that he would work for Laban for seven years in return for Rachel. Laban agreed and Jacob served him for seven years.

At the end of the seven years Laban hosted a great wedding feast. As night fell at the end of the feast, he led the veiled bride to Jacob's tent. That night they consummated the marriage. But when morning came, "Jacob was amazed: it was Leah!" (Genesis 29:25).

Jacob immediately confronted Laban, asking, "How could you do this to me?"

Laban simply replied, "It is not the custom in our country to marry off a younger daughter before an older one."

But not to worry, he said: Jacob could marry Rachel, too, in return for seven more years of service to Laban. But he didn't have to wait seven years for his bride; he married Rachel a week later.

So Jacob had two wives. But not just two wives but also their maidservants. Leah began to have children immediately, but Rachel did not. So Rachel gave her maidservant Bilhah to Jacob to be a surrogate mother, just as Sarai had done when she gave Hagar to Abram. Then, when Leah stopped having children, she gave her maidservant Zilpah to Jacob.

The final five verses of Chapter 29 and the first twenty-four verses of Chapter 30 of Genesis tell us that Jacob was a pretty happy man as four women vied to become mothers of his children. At one point, Leah traded some mandrakes (an herb thought to promote conception) to Rachel in return for her turn to sleep with Jacob that night.

Eventually, Leah gave birth to six sons—Reuben, Simeon, Levi, Judah, Issachar, and Zebulun—and a daughter, Dinah; Rachel had two sons, Joseph and Benjamin; Bilhah had two sons, Dan and Naphtali; and Zilpah had two sons, Gad and Asher.

Jacob remained in Mesopotamia for twenty

years before he had a falling-out with Laban, fled from him, and returned with his family to Canaan. After all that time, Esau was no longer angry with him and they had a peaceful reunion. Jacob settled first in Shechem, and then Bethel, where God changed his name to Israel, but then moved on.

Rachel was pregnant with Benjamin during this time and, as they neared Bethlehem, she went into a difficult labor. She died during the childbirth and Jacob buried her in Bethlehem. Her tomb remains a place of prayer for pregnant women to this day.

6

THE STORY OF JUDAH AND TAMAR

There are three women with the name Tamar in the Old Testament. Two of them were David's daughter and granddaughter. But this is the story of the first Tamar, the daughter-in-law of Judah, one of Jacob's twelve sons and the man for whom Judaism and the kingdom of Judah were named. The story, which is in Chapter 38 of Genesis, tells about some of the practices of the Israelites.

Judah married a Canaanite woman by whom he had three sons: Er, Onan and Shelah. When Er grew up, Judah got Tamar for him as his wife. Er died before he and Tamar could have children. Therefore, Judah told Onan that it was his duty to have children with Tamar in his brother's name. This was called the law of levirate, which the early Israelites considered important.

Onan, though, knowing that their children would not be counted as his, "wasted his seed on the ground" whenever he had intercourse with Tamar.

Because this act "greatly offended the Lord," the Bible says, God took his life.

Next Shelah was supposed to take his turn, but he was still a young boy. So Judah told Tamar to wait until Shelah grew up. Besides, Judah was afraid that Shelah would die as his two brothers did.

Years passed without Judah giving Shelah to Tamar. Judah's wife died, leaving him a widower. Then one day Tamar learned that Judah was going to a town called Timnah for the shearing of his sheep. She put on the clothing of a harlot, covered her face, and sat along the road on the way to Timnah.

When Judah came by and saw the harlot, he propositioned her. He offered her a kid from his flock if she would have sex with him. She agreed but asked for a pledge of some kind—his seal and cord and the staff he carried—until he sent the kid. Judah agreed. They had intercourse and Tamar conceived. When Judah sent his servant with the kid, naturally he couldn't find a harlot.

Three months later it became obvious that Tamar was pregnant. When word got to Judah, he became furious and cried, "Bring her out! She shall be burned!"

As they were bringing her out, Tamar sent word to her father-in-law, "It is by the man to whom these things belong that I am with child. Please verify whose seal and cord and whose staff these are."

Naturally, Judah recognized them as his. He said, "She is more in the right than I am, since I did not give her to my son Shelah." (There is nothing about the double standard that considered it all right for Judah to have had sex with a harlot but not all right for Tamar to have had sex with someone.)

Tamar bore twins who were named Perez and Zerah. All three are mentioned in the genealogy of Jesus in Matthew's Gospel (1:3).

The law of levirate (from the Latin *levir*, brother-in-law) was still recognized at the time of Jesus when the Sadducees tried to trick Jesus. They posited the idea that seven brothers married a woman but all died without children and asked whose wife she would be at the resurrection (Matthew 22:23-33).

7

THE STORY OF POTIPHAR'S WIFE

The story of the patriarch Joseph, in Chapters 37-50 of Genesis, has been praised for its remarkable integrity. Each step in the story lays the groundwork for the next and results in God's master plan to bring the Israelites to Egypt. For example, Joseph's imprisonment was necessary for him to win the Pharaoh's favor.

In those fourteen chapters, though, women appear only three times. One was the story about Tamar that we told in the previous chapter, a story that had nothing to do with Joseph's story. It probably was inserted to indicate the long lapse of time during which Joseph's family knew nothing of his life in Egypt. Another woman mentioned is Asenath, Joseph's wife and the mother of their sons Manasseh and Ephraim.

The third woman, Potiphar's wife, did figure in the story. Her story is in Chapter 39. Potiphar was Pharaoh's chief steward and the man who bought Joseph from the Ishmaelites to whom Joseph's brothers sold him. Potiphar took a liking to Joseph and put him in charge of his household and his possessions.

Joseph was a capable manager. With him in charge, Potiphar didn't have to worry about a thing except the food he ate. Because of Joseph, God blessed Potiphar's household and everything he owned.

Potiphar's wife, though, also took a liking to Joseph since he was "strikingly handsome." Eventually, she tried to seduce him, telling him quite bluntly, "Lie with me."

However, Joseph refused, telling her that her husband trusted him with all his possessions and didn't concern himself with anything in the house as long as Joseph was there. He said that Potiphar had withheld nothing from him except, of course, his wife. "How, then," he asked, "could I commit so great a wrong and thus stand condemned before God?"

Potiphar's wife continued to entice Joseph. He kept refusing, doing his best to avoid her.

One day, though, when Joseph came into the house to do his work, she grabbed him by his cloak and said, "Lie with me!" Joseph struggled to get away, leaving his cloak in her hand as he fled outside.

With that, Potiphar's wife screamed for the other household servants. When they came to see what was wrong, she showed them the cloak and accused Joseph of trying to have sex with her. When

Potiphar came home, she repeated the accusation, saying that his "Hebrew slave" had broken in on her but she screamed for the servants and Joseph ran away. She showed Joseph's cloak as her proof.

Potiphar believed his wife. He became enraged, seized Joseph and threw him into the jail where the royal prisoners were confined.

It might be nice to think that Potiphar eventually learned the truth, but that's not in the story. There was no redemption of Joseph in the eyes of Potiphar. But Joseph's imprisonment did lead to the recognition of his ability to interpret dreams, which led to his interpreting the Pharaoh's dream, and so on in this tale about Joseph.

8

MIRIAM AND ZIPPORAH

Unlike in Genesis, few women are mentioned in Exodus, Leviticus, Numbers and Deuteronomy, the remainder of the Jewish Torah. Those in this chapter are the exceptions.

Miriam was Moses' older sister. It was she who stayed behind to see what would happen when Moses' mother put the baby Moses, in a papyrus basket, among reeds on a river bank. Pharaoh's daughter found the baby and recognized it as one of the Hebrews' children.

At that, Miriam hurried to her and asked if she should get one of the Hebrew women to nurse the child for her. Pharaoh's daughter agreed, so Miriam got her own mother, who cared for Moses until he was weaned. Then his mother took him to Pharaoh's daughter, who adopted him as her son.

Miriam next appears after Moses has grown up and led the Israelites out of Egypt. After the Egyptian soldiers have drowned in the Red Sea, she led the Israelite women in singing the refrain to a triumphant song. At that point, the Bible calls Miriam a prophetess.

But things didn't always go well between Miriam and Moses. At one point, she and their brother Aaron became jealous of Moses and spoke out against him because he had married a Cushite woman. In his anger, God turned Miriam into a snow-white leper. When Moses saw her like that, he prayed to God to heal her. God did, but demanded that she be confined outside the camp for seven days.

Miriam died while the Israelite community was at Kadesh in the desert of Zin.

Zipporah was another important woman since she was Moses' wife and the mother of his children. She was one of seven daughters of a Midianite priest called at different times Reuel, Jethro and Hobab. Moses met her after he fled from Egypt as a young man after killing an Egyptian. The seven women were watering their sheep when some shepherds drove them away. Moses defended them and watered their flock for them. In gratitude, the priest invited Moses to live with them and gave him Zipporah as his wife. Presumably, Zipporah had nothing to say about the matter. The couple had two sons, Gershom and Eliezer.

After Moses was told by God to return to Egypt to lead the Israelites out, Zipporah and their son Gershom accompanied him. Along the way, she circumcised Gershom.

At some point while the Israelites were wandering in the desert, Moses sent Zipporah and their son back to Jethro. While the Israelites were by Mount Sinai, Jethro brought Zipporah and both boys back to Moses.

Other women mentioned in the Torah are Mahlah, Noah, Hoglah, Milcah and Tirzah, the five daughters of Zelophehad. He died without sons. The five women went to Moses and asked why their father's name should be withdrawn from his clan merely because he had no son and they asked for his property. Moses agreed and decreed that the property of a man who dies without a son should pass on to a daughter.

Later, though, that was modified. The daughter could marry only within a clan of her own ancestral tribe so that the property would remain within the clan.

9

RAHAB SAVES JOSHUA'S SPIES

Before launching his invasion of the Promised Land, Joshua wisely sent spies into the country. Two of them went to Jericho, where they lodged in a public house kept by a woman named Rahab. She is called a harlot but that doesn't necessarily mean that she was a prostitute. She might have been just the owner of a house where men lodged and the spies went there hoping to be undetected.

Somehow, though, word got out that spies were there, so the king of Jericho ordered Rahab to put the men out. Instead, she hid them on the roof of the house among stalks of flax. She admitted to the men who had come to arrest the spies that the men they were seeking had indeed been there, but she said that they left before the gate to the city was shut at dark. The king's men set out in pursuit and the city's gate was shut.

Rahab then went to the spies where they were hidden on the roof and told them that she knew that the Lord was going to give the Israelites the land. Jericho's inhabitants had heard of how the Lord had dried up the Red Sea and how the Israelites had defeated the Amorite kings Sihon and Og. They were in dread of the Israelites and discouraged. She said that she was going to help the spies and asked in return that, when Jericho was conquered, she and her family would be spared from death.

The spies guaranteed Rahab's safety. The house had been built into the city walls, so she let them down through a window with a rope. The spies told her that, when the invasion came, she was to tie a scarlet cord in that same window and to gather her family there. Then they escaped into the hills, until their pursuers gave up their chase.

The spies told Joshua what Rahab had done. Therefore, when the city was conquered and the Israelite soldiers were killing all of its inhabitants, Joshua ordered the two spies to go get Rahab and her family. They did, bringing her and all her kin to safety. Every other living thing—men and women, young and old, oxen, sheep and asses—were put to the sword.

Rahab and her family lived among the Israelites. She married a man named Salmon and their son was Boaz, the great-grandfather of King David. Rahab is included in the genealogy of Jesus in Matthew's Gospel.

Rahab is also mentioned in both the Letter to the Hebrews and the Letter of James in the New

Testament. In Hebrews she is included in the section that glorifies the faith of the ancient ancestors of the Jews: "By faith Rahab the harlot did not perish with the disobedient, for she had received the spies in peace" (Hebrews 11:31).

In James she is praised for her good works: "Was not Rahab the harlot justified by works when she welcomed the messengers and sent them out by a different route?" (James 2:25). She was, therefore, justified by both faith and good works.

10

THE STORY OF DEBORAH AND JAEL

The Book of Judges records the exploits of twelve Israelite heroes who exercised authority over the Israelites between the death of Joshua and the time of the priest Eli. During most of this time, the Israelites did not rule all of Palestine.

Deborah, the wife of Lappidoth, was one of those judges. She made it a practice to sit under a palm tree between Bethel and Ramah, a little north of Jerusalem, and there the Israelites came to her for judgment. We're not told how this woman became a judge in a patriarchal society, but we can assume that she must have demonstrated remarkable qualities of leadership.

During this period the Canaanite king Jabin ruled Palestine. Sisera was his general.

One day Deborah summoned Barak, who lived in Kedesh, north of the Sea of Galilee in the region of Naphtali. Deborah ordered Barak to round up ten thousand Naphtalis and Zebulunites, Israelites who lived between the Sea of Galilee and the Mediterranean Sea. She told Barak that the men should ascend Mount Tabor, located near the south end of the Sea of Galilee. Deborah said that she would then lead General Sisera there.

Barak agreed to do it only if Deborah went with him. All right, she said, but then Barak wouldn't get the glory in the expedition because Sisera would fall into the hands of a woman.

Deborah went back with Barak to Kedesh, where they raised their army and led them up Mount Tabor. When Sisera learned about it, he assembled nine hundred iron chariots and all of his force at the base of the mountain. Deborah ordered Barak to lead his men down the mountain because "the Lord marches before you."

He did and the Israelites routed Sisera's army. Sisera dismounted from his chariot and fled on foot while Barak pursued Sisera's army. Sisera made his way to the tent of Jael, wife of Heber, a Kenite, since the Kenite family and King Jabin were at peace.

Jael met Sisera and told him to hurry inside the tent, where she covered him with a rug. He asked for water, but Jael opened a jug of milk for him. Sisera told her to stand by the entrance of the tent and tell anyone who came that he wasn't there. Then he fell asleep.

As soon as she was sure he was asleep, Jael took a tent peg and a large mallet in her hands. She held the peg above Sisera's head and, with the mallet, drove the peg through his temple down into the ground, killing him instantly.

Soon Barak arrived, searching for Sisera. Jael calmly went out to meet him, took him to her tent, and showed him the body. Deborah's prophecy that Sisera would be felled by a woman had come true.

After this episode, Deborah sang a lengthy song, all of Chapter 5. It is considered an excellent example of early Hebrew poetry. It praised the tribes that formed the army against Sisera and we learn for the first time that it included more than those from Naphtali and Zebulon.

Shortly after that, King Jabin was destroyed and the land was at rest for forty years.

11

JEPHTHAH KILLS HIS DAUGHTER

If there is any episode in the Book of Judges that should shock us, it has to be the story of Jephthah and his daughter. The story clearly indicates the power and authority that men had over women and children during these days of the Israelites.

Jephthah led the Israelites in a battle against the Ammonites, who lived in modern Jordan. He was the son of Gilead and a harlot, and Gilead's wife insisted that he would inherit nothing from Gilead. So he fled from Palestine. Later, though, when the Ammonites were warring against the Israelites, the elders of Gilead persuaded Jephthah to lead them in battle. Jephthah first tried to make peace with the Ammonites, but to no avail, so he prepared for battle.

As his army was marching toward the battle, Jephthah made a vow to the Lord that, if God would deliver the Ammonites into his power, he would offer up as a holocaust whoever came out of the doors of his home to meet him when he returned in triumph. He clearly vowed to make a human sacrifice to God according to the custom of his pagan neighbors.

Naturally, his forces were successful and inflicted a severe defeat on the Ammonites. When he returned to his home, his beloved daughter was the first one to come running out of his house, happily playing the tambourine and dancing in celebration. She was his only child.

Alas, he had made a vow to God. He told his daughter about the vow and said that he couldn't retract it. Then, improbably, his daughter agreed that he had made a vow and would have to keep it.

She asked only that she be permitted to go away with her girl friends for two months "to mourn my virginity." For Israelite women, bearing children was a woman's greatest pride and responsibility and Jephthah's daughter asked to mourn the fact that she would have to die without bearing children.

Jephthah agreed and his daughter and her friends went away for two months. They returned and Jephthah killed her as a sacrifice to God. The Bible doesn't tell us how.

As we read this passage, my first question is always, "Where was her mother?" Is it possible that any mother would permit her husband to kill their daughter, whether or not he had made a vow to God? But this was a patriarchal society and a father had complete control over his wife and children.

A footnote in the New American Bible tells us that the inspired author of this book merely recorded the facts in this story; he didn't approve of the action. Even the God of the Old Testament didn't require human sacrifice to him and it was wrong for Jephthah to make the vow.

The Book of Judges closes this episode by telling us that it became a custom in Israel for Israelite women to go yearly to mourn the daughter of Jephthah for four days of the year.

12

THE MOTHER OF SAMSON

Chapter 13 of the Book of Judges says that the Philistines ruled over the Israelites for forty years. The number forty is used often in Scripture, usually as a way of saying a long time. The Philistines were the ancestors of today's Palestinians, who had settled originally in Gaza. The Israelites fought them during much of the Old Testament.

Manoah was an Israelite from the clan of the Danites. Dan was the northernmost tribe of Israel, located north of the Sea of Galilee. Manoah and his wife had been unable to have children.

One day while she was working in a field, an angel appeared to Manoah's wife (her name is never mentioned). He told her that she would bear a son, and a special son at that. He was to be consecrated to God from the womb and no razor was to touch his head because he would begin the deliverance of Israel from the Philistines. And the woman, too, was to abstain from wine or strong drink and eat nothing unclean.

The angel was telling her that the child was to be raised as a nazirite, as John the Baptist was to be raised centuries later.

Naturally, Manoah's wife hurried to tell her husband what she had just experienced. After he heard what had happened, Manoah prayed that the man of God would come back to tell them what they were to do for the boy who was to be born. How should they raise this special child?

God heard Manoah's prayer and sent the angel back to the woman. She immediately rushed to get Manoah so he could hear what the angel had to say. The angel basically repeated himself, not saying anything specific about how the child should be raised, but saying, as he had before, that Manoah's wife was to abstain from drinking wine and strong drink and from eating anything unclean.

The woman didn't seem to be nearly as curious as Manoah, who wanted to know the man's name "that we may honor you when your words come true." The angel didn't tell his name, saying only that it was mysterious, above human understanding. When asked to stay and eat with them, the angel refused, but said that Manoah might offer a kid as a holocaust to God.

When Manoah and his wife offered the kid with a cereal offering, the flames from the fire rose to the sky. While the couple watched, the angel ascended in the flame.

Manoah became frightened. "We will certainly die," he said, "for we have seen God."

His wife, though, was more sensible. She pointed out that, if God had meant to kill them, he wouldn't have accepted the holocaust and cereal offering they had just sacrificed. Besides, she might have reminded her husband, how would she bear a special son as the angel said?

She did bear a son, of course, and named him Samson. He was the strongest man in the Old Testament, accomplishing great feats.

13

SAMSON'S PHILISTINE WIFE

Quick, who was Samson's wife? If you automatically said Delilah, you're wrong. I'll write about Delilah in the next chapter, but she was not Samson's wife.

Samson went down to Timnah, which is due west of Jerusalem, where he saw a Philistine woman who pleased him. Returning home, he asked his parents to get her for him as his wife. They tried to persuade him to get a wife among the Israelites, but Samson simply repeated that the woman pleased him. So the three of them went down to Timnah and successfully made a bargain for the Philistine woman.

As part of the wedding celebration, Samson gave a feast—a seven-day feast. The father of the bride appointed thirty Philistine men as Samson's "companions" for the feast. Samson proposed a riddle for them and made a bet. The loser would have to provide thirty linen tunics and thirty sets of garments for the winner.

The riddle Samson proposed was: "Out of the

eater came forth food, and out of the strong came forth sweetness."

The riddle had been set up on Samson's trip to Timnah. A lion had attacked him, but he was able to kill it with his bare hands. When he returned to marry the Philistine woman, he stopped to see the remains of the lion and found a swarm of bees and honey in the lion's carcass. The answer to the riddle, therefore, would be a lion and honey.

Naturally, none of the thirty "companions" could solve the riddle, so they coaxed Samson's wife to learn the answer for them. They threatened to burn her and her family if she didn't. So she used all of her womanly wiles to learn the answer. Samson said that he hadn't even told his parents, so why would he tell her? But she wept until Samson finally gave her the answer.

On the seventh day of the banquet, the men told Samson, "What is sweeter than honey, and what is stronger than a lion?"

Samson knew immediately how they learned the answer. He said, "If you had not plowed with my heifer, you would not have solved my riddle." He stormed out of the house, went to Ashkelon, killed thirty Philistines, and brought their garments back to the men in Timnah. Then he went off to his own family in anger.

Sometime later, Samson returned to try to see his wife, only to learn that her father, assuming that Samson no longer wanted anything to do with her, had married her off to the best man at Samson's wedding. He offered Samson her younger sister instead. This really infuriated Samson. He caught three hundred foxes, tied their tails together and tied a torch between each pair of tails. He then set them loose and they burned up the Philistines' standing grain, vineyards and olive orchards.

When the Philistines were told that this had been done by Samson because his wife was given to his best man, they retaliated by burning Samson's wife and family.

14

DELILAH BETRAYS SAMSON

If you think about a man being unlucky in love, could you find a better example than Samson? When reading about him, though, one has to conclude that he must have been a stupid brute of a man.

In the previous chapter I wrote about the way Samson's wife betrayed him. She had a horrible end when the Philistines, in retribution for Samson's destroying Philistine vineyards and olive orchards, burned her and her family. This further enraged Samson, who became a one-man army. At one point, Scripture says he killed a thousand men using the jawbone of an ass.

Later, Samson fell in love with Delilah. By this time, the Philistines were determined to capture Samson, so they told Delilah to learn the secret of his great strength.

First Samson told Delilah that he would be as weak as any other man if he were bound with seven fresh bowstrings. So Delilah bound him with seven fresh bowstrings while she had men lying in wait.

But when she called, "The Philistines are upon you, Samson," he snapped the strings as though they were thread.

She tried again. This time Samson said that he would be weak if he were tied with ropes with which no work had been done. So Delilah bound him with new ropes. And once again, when she called, "The Philistines are upon you, Samson," he broke the new ropes as though they were thread.

Delilah tried a third time. This time Samson said that he would be weak if his seven locks of hair were woven into a web and fastened with a pin. So, while Samson slept, Delilah wove his hair. And once again, Samson was able to pull out both the weaver's pin and the web.

Wouldn't you think that Samson might think by now that just perhaps Delilah didn't really have his best interests at heart? But Delilah cooed, "How can you say that you love me when you do not confide in me?" She kept at him until he finally told her the truth: No razor had ever touched his hair because he had been consecrated to God. If his hair was shaved, he'd be weak.

So Delilah had Samson sleep on her lap. While he was asleep she called for a man to come in and shave his head. (He must have been a sound sleeper.) This time when she called, "The Philistines are upon you, Samson!" he couldn't get away as he had before. The Philistines seized him and gouged out his eyes. He was taken to Gaza where he was put in prison.

The Scriptures don't tell us what happened to Delilah after that. But, of course, we know what happened to Samson. Sometime later, after his hair began to grow back, he was taken to the Philistine temple where about three thousand men made fun of him. He grasped the two middle columns on which the temple rested, pushed hard, and the temple fell on him and all the Philistines who were in the temple.

15

THE STORY OF RUTH AND NAOMI

The Book of Ruth tells a delightful story about the faithfulness of Ruth to her mother-in-law Naomi.

Naomi, her husband Elimelech, and their sons Mahlon and Chilion moved from Bethlehem to Moab, east of the Dead Sea. The sons married Moabite women, Orpah and Ruth. Elimelech died shortly after they moved, and both Mahlon and Chilion died after they had been in Moab for about ten years.

Naomi decided to move back to Bethlehem and told her daughters-in-law to return to their parents' homes so they could find new husbands. Orpah did so, but Ruth said, "Wherever you go I will go, wherever you lodge I will lodge, your people shall be my people, and your God my God. Wherever you die I will die, and there be buried."

After arriving back in Bethlehem, Ruth decided to glean grain in one of the fields because Israelite law permitted poor widows to pick up any grain missed during harvest time. Boaz, the owner of the field, asked who the girl was. When he learned that she was Naomi's daughter-in-law, he told her to continue to glean in his field because he had heard about what she had done for Naomi.

When Ruth told Naomi about Boaz, Naomi realized that he was a relative of her husband Elimelech. She instructed Ruth to bathe and anoint herself, and then to go down to the threshing floor where Boaz would be sleeping. After Boaz was asleep, Naomi told Ruth, she should uncover a place at his feet and lie there.

Ruth did as Naomi instructed. In the middle of the night, Boaz awakened to find Ruth at his feet and asked who was there. Ruth identified herself and asked him to "spread the corner of your cloak over me," thus asking him to become her protector according to the duty of a near kinsman (see Deuteronomy 25:5 and Exodus 16:8).

Boaz said that he would do as she asked, but noted that she had another relative who was more closely related to her. He told her to remain there that night. In the morning, she left while it was still dark so as not to cause scandal.

Boaz then asked Naomi's nearer relative to meet with him and ten elders of the city who would serve as witnesses of a proposed business transaction. He told the relative that Naomi planned to put up for sale a piece of property that belonged to Elimelech and asked if he wanted to claim it as next of kin. The man said that he did wish to do so. OK, Boaz told him. However, he said, if he did, he would also have to take Ruth the Moabite and raise up a family for the departed Elimelech on his estate. The relative then passed and told Boaz that he could exercise the claim.

Boaz married Ruth. They had a son, Obed, who became the grandfather of King David. Boaz had been a descendent of Perez, whose wife Tamar was, like Ruth, a Gentile. Both women are listed in the genealogy of Jesus in Matthew's Gospel.

16

PENINNAH AND HANNAH

No man should have two wives. It always seems to lead to trouble. But, as we've seen in this book, it wasn't unusual during Old Testament times. In fact, some biblical characters had more than two wives—as we'll see in the next three chapters.

Elkanah was one of those men with two wives—Peninnah and Hannah. And wouldn't you know, Peninnah had children but Hannah didn't. And don't think that Penninnah didn't rub it in to Hannah. She constantly reminded Hannah that the Lord had made her barren. For her part, Hannah was quite sensitive about the matter, weeping and refusing to eat.

During these days before David conquered Jerusalem, the Israelites worshiped at Shiloh, in the hill country of Ephraim a little south of modern Nablus. Once when Elkanah, Peninnah and Hannah were there, Hannah went to the temple and prayed her heart out, weeping copiously. She promised God that, if she would have a son, she would give him to the Lord and that he would live as a nazirite, never drinking wine or liquor or having his hair cut. Her lips moved as she prayed, but her voice couldn't be heard.

It happened that the priest Eli was there at the time. As he watched Hannah's lips moving, he thought she was drunk. So he confronted her and admonished her to sober up and stop making a spectacle of herself. Hannah assured Eli that she wasn't drunk, just unhappy and pouring out her troubles to God. Eli told her to go in peace.

Sure enough, Hannah conceived a child and bore a son whom they called Samuel. Once the child had been weaned, they kept the promise Hannah had made and took him to the temple. Hannah approached Eli and reminded him who she was. She told him that she was the woman whom he thought drunk, who was praying for a child. Her prayer was answered, so she was now giving him to the Lord. She left Samuel with Eli.

Then Hannah prayed a great prayer about the greatness of God that is similar to Mary's Magnificat. She prayed, "My heart exults in the Lord, my horn is exalted in my God. I have swallowed up my enemies; I rejoice in my victory. There is no Holy One like the Lord; there is no Rock like our God."

Other parts of her prayer say, "The bows of the mighty are broken, while the tottering gird on strength. The well-fed hire themselves out for bread, while the hungry batten on spoil. The barren wife bears seven sons, while the mother of many languishes." Mary prayed the same thing during her visitation to Elizabeth.

As Samuel grew up, Hannah naturally didn't forget him. She made clothing for him that she would bring each time she and Elkanah went to Shiloh to offer sacrifices. Each time Eli would bless the couple saying, "May the Lord repay you with children from this woman for the gift she has made to the Lord!"

God did indeed repay Hannah. She gave birth to three more sons and two daughters while Samuel grew up in the service of the Lord.

17

DAVID'S FIRST WIFE, MICHAL

Michal, the daughter of King Saul, was smitten with David. When Saul learned of it, he was glad because he thought he could use Michal to kill David, whom he saw as a rival.

Therefore, he offered Michal to David as his wife. The bridal price was the foreskins of one hundred Philistines. Saul hoped that, while David was trying to get them, the Philistines would kill him. But David brought back two hundred foreskins, counted them out before the king, and claimed Michal in marriage. (Some things in the Bible are simply distasteful.)

That made Saul even more determined to kill David. He sent guards to David's house with orders to kill him in the morning. Michal, knowing what her father had in mind, saved her husband by lowering David down through a window. Then she put an idol, with a net of goat's hair on its head, in the bed. When the soldiers burst in the next morning, she told them that David was sick.

The messengers reported back to Saul, who

ordered them to bring David back, bed and all, so he could kill him. That's when they found that Michal had deceived them. Naturally, Saul was furious with Michal, who said that David had threatened to kill her if she hadn't helped him escape.

David was on the run from Saul for a long time. Saul gave Michal in marriage to a man named Paltiel. After Saul's death, David lived in Hebron, where he had other wives: Ahinoam, Abigail, Maacah, Higgith, Abital, and Eglah. They all bore him children.

Eventually, David decided that he also wanted Michal back, so he sent Abner to get her for him. David sent messengers to Ishbaal, Saul's son, reminding him that David had paid two hundred foreskins for Michal. Therefore, Ishbaal took her away from Paltiel and sent her with Abner back to David. Paltiel followed her, weeping, until Abner sent him back.

After David conquered Jerusalem, he took more wives and concubines. Michal, although his first wife, was basically just part of the harem.

Then came the day when David brought the Ark of the Covenant to Jerusalem. It was a joyous occasion and David, clad only in a loincloth, danced with abandon in front of the Ark. Michal, though, looking through a window, saw David's performance and felt contempt for him.

As soon as David entered his home, Michal confronted him: "How the king of Israel has honored himself today," she said, "exposing himself to the view of the slave girls of his followers, as a commoner might do!"

David rejected her scorn. "I was dancing before the Lord," he told her. "As the Lord lives, who preferred me to your father and his whole family…, not only will I make merry before the Lord, but I will demean myself even more. I will be lowly in your esteem, but in the esteem of the slave girls you spoke of I will be honored."

From then on, David had nothing to do with Michal.

18

DAVID'S THIRD WIFE, ABIGAIL

"He did what?!" Abigail said to one of the servants.

"David sent messengers to your husband Nabal to ask for some food for him and his men, but Nabal flew at them screaming," the servant repeated. "He yelled, 'Who is David? Nowadays there are many servants who run away from their masters. Must I take my bread, my wine, my meat that I have slaughtered for my own shearers, and give them to men who come from I know not where?'

"Yet these men had been very good to us while we were shepherding our master's three thousand sheep and one thousand goats while we lived among them in the open country," the servant told Abigail.

This was during the time when David was a fugitive from King Saul.

Perhaps Nabal didn't know who David was, but Abigail did, and she knew that he was not a man to be trifled with. She quickly had the servants get together two hundred loaves of bread, two skins of wine, five dressed sheep, five measures of roasted grain, one hundred bunches of raisins, and two hundred cakes of figs. She ordered the servants to take them to David, while she would follow.

David had indeed planned to punish Nabal for his rudeness and refusal to feed his men. He had taken four hundred of his followers and they were on the road to Carmel, where Nabal and Abigail lived. He vowed to kill Nabal and all the males who belonged to him.

As soon as Abigail saw David and his men, she dismounted from the ass on which she was riding and fell prostrate on the ground before David. "My lord, let the blame be mine," she exclaimed. "Let not my lord pay attention to that worthless man Nabal, for he is just like his name." ("Nabal" in Hebrew means "a fool.")

Abigail continued at length, praising David and predicting that God would establish a lasting dynasty for David. She asked him to accept the food she had brought with her and to spare Nabal so that, after God had appointed David as commander over Israel, he would not have it on his conscience that he had shed innocent blood.

David was impressed. He praised her for her good judgment for meeting him because otherwise, he said, "by dawn Nabal would not have a single man or boy left alive." He told Abigail to go home in peace.

When she got back home she found Nabal

drunk during a drinking party in their home. So she waited until the next day to tell him what had happened. When he realized what he had done, he was stricken physically. He died ten days later.

When David learned that Nabal had died, he sent a proposal of marriage to Abigail, who immediately got up, mounted an ass, and followed David's messengers along with her five maids. She became David's third wife, after King Saul gave David's first wife, Michal, to another man and after his second wife, Ahinoam. Later David married more women.

19

THE BEAUTIFUL BATHSHEBA

Did Bathsheba know that King David would be able to see her while she bathed on the rooftop of her home? The Second Book of Samuel gives no indication that she did, but I have looked down from the site of David's palace and can easily understand how easy it would have been to see someone bathing on the roof of a building below.

The Bible, though, only tells us that David did see a beautiful woman, Bathsheba, the wife of Uriah the Hittite, bathing one afternoon. It was a spring day when David's army was battling the Ammonites, and Uriah was with the army since he was the armor-bearer of Joab, David's general.

David sent messengers to Bathsheba's home to bring her to him. Then he had sex with her. Surely in our day the question would arise whether or not it was consensual, but David was king and Bathsheba really had no choice.

Bathsheba returned to her home. Within a month it was clear that she was pregnant, so she sent the information to David, "I am with child."

Bathsheba probably had no inkling about what happened next until she received the news that her husband was dead. First David recalled Uriah from the battlefield and tried to get him to go to his home where he would make love to his wife and then believe that Bathsheba's child was his. But when Uriah didn't return to his home after two days in Jerusalem, David gave instructions to Joab to put Uriah in the front, where the fighting was the fiercest, and then to pull back so that Uriah would be killed by the Ammonites. It happened just as David planned.

When Bathsheba received the news of Uriah's death, she naturally mourned because there is no reason to believe that she didn't love him. But after the time for mourning was over, David again sent for her. She became another of David's wives.

She bore the son she had conceived. But God was displeased with David's sin and punished him by striking the child with a fatal illness. The Bible tells us about the anguish David felt while the baby was dying, but certainly Bathsheba felt just as bad—probably worse, since she was the baby's mother.

At least the Bible says that David comforted Bathsheba after the baby's death. They slept together again and Bathsheba conceived another child. This time the baby lived. They named the baby Solomon. As he grew up, David assured him that he would succeed him as king of Israel.

When David grew old, though, some of his other sons had other ideas. Adonijah, son of David's wife Haggith, made plans to have him crowned king. He went so far as to slaughter a great number of oxen and sheep for a feast.

When the prophet Nathan learned about it, he and Bathsheba took the news to David, who assured them that he meant for Solomon to succeed him. Those faithful to Solomon then anointed him as king.

20

THE RAPE OF TAMAR

When I wrote about Judah and Tamar in the sixth chapter of this book, I said that there are three Tamars in the Old Testament. In this chapter I'll tell you about the Tamar who was King David's daughter. It's not a pretty story, but it demonstrates just how dysfunctional David's family was.

Tamar was the daughter of Maacah, David's fourth wife after Michal, Ahinoam and Abigail. She was the full sister of Absalom and, of course, had numerous half brothers and half sisters.

One of them was Amnon, the eldest of David's children. He fell in love with Tamar, so stricken that he became ill since he didn't think it possible to consummate his love. One of his friends, a cousin named Jonadab (son of David's brother Shimeah), asked what was wrong, and Amnon confessed his love for Tamar.

Jonadab advised Amnon to pretend to be sick and, when his father, David, came to visit him, to suggest that it would help if Tamar would prepare some food for him. Amnon did as Jonadab suggested. He pretended to be sick, and when David came to visit him, he asked him to send Tamar to prepare some fried cakes for him. Suspecting nothing, David asked Tamar to prepare some nourishment for Amnon.

When Tamar went to Amnon's house, she found him in bed. While he watched, she kneaded some dough, twisted it into cakes, and fried them. Amnon ordered all his servants out and then asked Tamar to bring the cakes into his bedroom. When she did so, he seized her and commanded, "Come! Lie with me, my sister!"

Tamar resisted. "No, my brother!" she said. "Do not shame me! That is an intolerable crime in Israel. Do not commit this insensate deed. Where would I take my shame? And you would be a discredited man in Israel."

Ignoring her plea, Amnon raped her. Then, once his lust was satiated, he felt a hatred for her that surpassed the love he had had. He commanded her to leave.

Tamar tore the long tunic in which she had been clothed, put ashes on her head, and went away crying loudly. Absalom heard her and quickly realized what had happened. "Has your brother Amnon been with you?" he asked. "Be still now, my sister; he is your brother. Do not take this affair to heart."

King David learned what had happened

and was angry, but did nothing since Amnon, his first-born, was his favorite. Absalom, though, hated Amnon for what he had done to Tamar.

Nothing more happened for two years. Then one day, at the time of year when the sheep were sheared, Absalom prepared a banquet for his brothers. He instructed his servants, "When Amnon is merry with wine and I say to you, 'Kill Amnon,' put him to death." The servants did as Absalom ordered and Absalom had revenge for what Amnon had done to Tamar.

Absalom, afraid of what David might do, fled for three years. We don't know what happened to Tamar.

21

THE QUEEN OF SHEBA

The queen of Sheba is a mysterious figure in the Old Testament. Chapter 10 of the First Book of Kings narrates her visit to King Solomon. She arrived in Jerusalem with a large retinue, including camels bearing spices, a large amount of gold and other precious stones.

The reign of King Solomon was by far the most prosperous period in Israel's history, so it's natural that other countries wanted to trade with Israel. Sheba for centuries was the leading principality in what is now Yemen, and, according to eighth-century B.C. Assyrian inscriptions, there were sometimes women rulers among the Arabs.

If this caravan came from modern Yemen, it had traveled a great distance. The visit probably had mostly to do with trade and commerce, but the Bible uses it to stress Solomon's wisdom. It probably was a very large caravan since the Bible says that "never again did anyone bring such an abundance of spices as the queen of Sheba gave to King Solomon."

In return, Solomon "gave the queen of Sheba everything she desired and asked for, besides such presents as were given her from Solomon's royal bounty." It seems obvious that he was enthralled by her visit.

The queen was equally charmed. In fact, the Bible says that she was breathless when she saw Solomon's "great wisdom, the palace he had built, the food at his table, the seating of his ministers, the attendance and garb of his waiters, his banquet service, and the holocausts he offered in the temple of the Lord." Solomon obviously knew how to do things right.

When she recovered her breath, the queen of Sheba told Solomon that when she first heard about his deeds and wisdom she didn't believe the report, but now that she had seen it with her own eyes she discovered that the report didn't tell her the half. She questioned him about every subject in which she was interested and Solomon was able to explain everything she asked about.

So the queen said, "Your wisdom and prosperity surpass the report I heard. Happy are your men, happy these servants of yours, who stand before you always and listen to your wisdom. Blessed be the Lord, your God, whom it has pleased to place you on the throne of Israel."

After making their trade, the queen returned to Sheba.

This same chapter in the First Book of Kings

then devotes sixteen verses to describing the wealth of Solomon's kingdom. It says that he "surpassed in riches and wisdom all the kings of the earth. And the whole world sought audience with Solomon, to hear from him the wisdom which God had put in his heart."

Among his possessions were "seven hundred wives of princely rank and three hundred concubines." His celebrated wisdom, though, did not keep him from turning his heart to strange gods, by adoring the gods of some of his non-Israelite wives. Therefore, God told Solomon that, in punishment, he would divide his kingdom—after his death.

22

JEZEBEL, AHAB'S WICKED WIFE

Jezebel was evil. The daughter of the king of Sidon, modern Lebanon, she was the wife of Ahab, king of the northern kingdom of Israel, which included Samaria and Galilee. She brought the worship of Baal and Asherah to Israel, and enticed Ahab to build a temple to Baal. She murdered Israel's prophets. Ahab's vizier Obadiah managed to save one hundred of them by hiding them in two caves.

Elijah was Jezebel's mortal enemy. He confronted Ahab and told him to bring the four hundred fifty prophets of Baal and the four hundred prophets of Asherah to Mount Carmel. He told them to place a bull on an altar and call upon Baal to send down fire to burn it. The prophets prayed, danced, and cut themselves, while Elijah taunted them. Then Elijah put his bull on an altar and had them pour water over it until water lapped around the altar. He called on God, and the Lord's fire came down and consumed the holocaust, wood, stones and water. Then Elijah had the crowd seize the four hundred fifty prophets of Baal and he slit their throats.

After Ahab reported to Jezebel what had happened, she sent a messenger to Elijah telling him that she would kill him. Elijah fled to the kingdom of Judah.

Sometime later, while Ahab and Jezebel were in their palace at Jezreel, Ahab tried to buy the vineyard of his neighbor Naboth. Naboth refused to sell it. Jezebel wrote letters to the elders and nobles in Jezreel telling them to get two scoundrels to accuse Naboth of having cursed God and king. They obeyed, led Naboth out of the city and stoned him to death.

When Jezebel learned that Naboth was dead, she told Ahab to go take possession of the vineyard. However, he met Elijah while he was on his way. Elijah told Ahab that God would punish him by having dogs lick up his blood where they licked up the blood of Naboth. Furthermore, he predicted, dogs would devour Jezebel. Later the prophet Elisha, who succeeded Elijah, repeated the prediction.

Three years later, King Ahab of Israel and King Jehoshaphat of Judah went to war against Aram, modern Syria. A lucky arrow struck Ahab between the joints of his breastplate, and he died, his blood flowing to the bottom of his chariot. After they returned to Samaria and the chariot was washed, dogs licked up his blood.

Ahaziah, Ahab's and Jezebel's son, succeeded Ahab, but he ruled Israel for only two years. He was succeeded by his brother Joram, who reigned for twelve years. He was murdered by Jehu, chosen by God to return Israel to worship of the true God. Jehu rode into Jezreel, where Jezebel put on makeup and fixed her hair. When Jehu saw Jezebel at an upstairs window, he sent eunuchs to throw her down. They did, and her blood spurted against the wall and against the horses.

Hours later, when Jehu sent orders to have Jezebel buried, the attendants discovered that dogs had devoured her.

23

ATHALIAH AND JEHOSHEBA

The kings and queens of the kingdoms of Israel and Judah during the ninth century B.C. were especially ruthless and bloodthirsty. In the previous chapter I wrote about Jezebel, the wife of King Ahab of Israel and the enemy of the prophet Elijah. She was finally killed on orders from Jehu, who then reigned over Israel for twenty-eight years. In the eyes of the authors of the Bible, Jehu was a good guy. He destroyed the temple of Baal that Ahab had built.

The story now shifts to the kingdom of Judah. (I realize that the similarity of the names of the characters in this chapter makes it difficult to keep track of the action, but I'll do my best.)

Athaliah was either Ahab's sister or his and Jezebel's daughter. She married King Jehoram of Judah and became the mother of Ahaziah, who became king of Judah in 841 B.C. Like Ahab and Jezebel, Athaliah was a worshiper of Baal.

Through treachery, Jehu killed Ahaziah, and not only Ahaziah but forty-two of his kinsmen.

Ahaziah was buried in Jerusalem, the capital of the kingdom of Judah.

When Athaliah learned that her son Ahaziah was dead, she began to kill off the whole royal family in Judah so that she could rule the kingdom.

Enter Jehosheba. She was the daughter of King Jehoram and the sister of the slain Ahaziah. She was also the wife of Jehoiada, the high priest. When she discovered that Athaliah was murdering all the male members of the royal family, she saved her nephew Joash, Ahaziah's youngest son, then one year old. She took him from the bedroom where the other princes were about to be slain. Jehosheba and Jehoiada hid Joash in the temple for six years.

Athaliah was unaware that one of the princes had survived the massacre. She ruled as queen of Judah for the next six years.

When Joash was seven, the priest Jehoiada summoned the captains of the guard to the temple and showed them the late king's son, Joash. He instructed them on how they were to protect King Joash. Then Jehoiada led Joash out to the altar in the temple and put the king's crown and insignia on him. The people proclaimed him king and shouted, "Long live the king!"

Athaliah heard the noise and hurried to the temple to see what was going on. When she saw Joash standing at the pillar of the temple with a crown on his head, and all the people rejoicing, she tore her garments and cried, "Treason, treason!"

Jehoiada instructed the captains in command of the force, "Bring her outside," because he had given orders that she was not to be killed in the temple. She was roughly led out of the temple to the palace's horse gate, where she was put to death.

Joash was to rule Judah for forty years. The temple of Baal in Judah was destroyed, as the one in Israel had been destroyed by Jehu, and the people of Judah returned to the worship of the true God—temporarily.

24

THE STORY OF SARAH AND TOBIAH

Sarah had been married seven times, but each time, on their wedding night, the demon Asmodeus had killed her husbands. Now she was to be married again, this time to Tobiah, who had just arrived with a man named Azariah and had claimed her for his wife because he was her nearest relative.

The love story of Tobiah and Sarah in the Book of Tobit is a religious novel set during the time after the fall of the Northern Kingdom of Israel to Assyria. Tobiah has traveled from Nineveh, in modern Iraq, to Media, modern Iran, to get some money that his father Tobit had left with a man named Gabael. Azariah, Tobiah's companion, is really the archangel Raphael, sent by God in answer to prayers said at the same time by Tobit and Sarah. Both had prayed for death.

In Sarah's case, it was after a maid had accused Sarah of strangling her husbands. In great distress, she went to her room intending to hang herself. But realizing the pain this would cause her father Raguel, she begged God to let her die.

As Tobiah and Raphael traveled to Media and neared Ecbatana, Raphael told Tobiah that they would stay with Raguel that night. He also told him about Sarah, Raguel and his wife Edna's only child, and Tobiah's closest relative. Raguel would know that, according to the Book of Moses, Tobiah had the right to marry his daughter.

They arrived at Raguel and Edna's home, introduced themselves, and were welcomed joyfully. During dinner, Tobiah told Raphael to ask Raguel to let him marry Sarah. Raguel answered that Tobiah had the right to her, but he should understand that she had been wed seven times and her husbands never survived their wedding night.

Tobiah said that he still wanted to marry her, so Raguel called Sarah and gave her to Tobiah. Edna brought a scroll and the men drew up a wedding contract.

That night, Sarah awaited her new husband in the bedroom. When Tobiah arrived, he brought with him the liver and heart from a fish he had caught during his journey. He placed them on burning embers and the horrible odor repelled the demon Asmodeus, who had been awaiting Tobiah. The demon fled to the desert of Egypt. Raphael pursued him, bound him hand and foot, and then returned.

Before going to bed, Tobiah and Sarah prayed together, calling for God's mercy on them and asking him to allow them to live together to a happy old age.

Raguel, expecting the worst, had his servants dig a grave for Tobiah. Then he sent a servant in to see how the couple was. The servant reported that they were sleeping peacefully. Raguel had the servants fill in the grave.

Tobiah and Sarah returned to Nineveh and lived happily ever after. They had seven sons. After the deaths of Tobit and his wife Anna, they returned to Ecbatana and were living there when they learned about the destruction of Nineveh.

25

JUDITH DEFEATS HOLOFERNES

The Book of Judith is another religious novel in the Old Testament. The events described were not part of the Israelites' history. It was written as a pious reflection on God's abiding presence among the Jews. The name "Judith" means "Jewess."

Holofernes, the commander of the armies of King Nebuchadnezzar, has led an overwhelming force against the vassal states that refused to help in the Assyrian war against the Medes. The Jews stubbornly resist Holofernes at Bethulia. Holofernes lays siege to the town, cuts off the water supply, and begins to starve the people. After thirty-four days, the Jews are ready to surrender.

Judith is the widow of a man named Manasseh, "beautifully formed and lovely to behold." But for three years and four months she had worn sackcloth and widow's clothing. She was known to be a God-fearing woman.

When she learned that the elders of Bethulia were ready to surrender, she called them to her house and gave them a lengthy speech about how God was with the Jews as long as they didn't offend him. She asked them to let her out of the city and not to surrender for five days. The Lord would rescue Israel by her hand, she said.

The elders agreed. Judith took off her widow's clothing and anointed her body with rich ointment. She put on the festive attire she had worn while she was married. She arranged her hair attractively and put on her finest jewelry. As the story says, "She made herself very beautiful, to captivate the eyes of all the men who should see her."

Thus she left Bethulia with her maid and made her way to the enemy camp. When she was captured, she asked to be taken to Holofernes, who was taken by her beauty. She praised the great King Nebuchadnezzar and said that she would help Holofernes defeat the Jews.

Holofernes gave her a room next to his and asked her to join him at table, but she insisted on eating only the provisions her maid had brought in a food pouch. She asked only to be permitted to go out each night to wash and say her prayers. Holofernes ordered his men not to hinder her coming and going.

On the fourth day, Holofernes gave a banquet and asked Judith to join him. She did, after putting on all her best clothing and jewelry. During the banquet Holofernes drank more wine than he had ever drunk before. Then the servants withdrew, leaving Holofernes and Judith alone.

Holofernes had passed out. Judith took his sword and, after saying a prayer, struck him twice in the neck, cutting off his head. She quickly took his head and passed it to her maid, who put it in her food pouch. Then the two women went out as they were accustomed to do for prayer. Unhindered by Holofernes's men, they made their way back to Bethulia.

With Holofernes dead, his army went into confusion and the Jews overwhelmed them.

26

ESTHER SAVES THE JEWS

The Book of Esther is another fictional book, set in Persia at the time of King Xerxes (485-464 B.C.), called King Ahasuerus in the book. The king became displeased when his queen, Vashti, refused to come to a drunken banquet. He banished the queen and then searched the kingdom for beautiful virgins to replace her.

Esther, an orphan who was being cared for by her uncle Mordecai, was one of the virgins brought to the royal court. The book says that she "was beautifully formed and lovely to behold." After each girl in the harem had visited the king, he chose Esther and made her queen in place of Vashti. On Mordecai's advice, she kept secret the fact that she was Jewish.

Haman was King Ahasuerus's second in command. When he passed on the street, all the people were to bow down to him. But Mordecai, as a good Jew, refused to bow down, keeping such homage for God alone. This angered Haman. He built a gibbet on which to hang Mordecai.

When he learned that Mordecai was a Jew, Haman told King Ahasuerus that there were people in his kingdom who did not obey his laws. He proposed that all these people be rounded up for execution on a single day. The king issued the decree.

Mordecai put on sackcloth and ashes and walked through the city crying out loudly. Esther sent one of the eunuchs, Hathach, to learn why Mordecai was behaving like that. Mordecai told him what was about to happen to the Jews and asked Esther to appeal to the king.

Esther replied, through Hathach, that it was well known that anyone who went to the king without being summoned could suffer the penalty of death. Mordecai replied that she should not think that she alone would escape what was about to happen.

Esther sent word for all the Jews to fast on her behalf. She and her maids also fasted and prayed for three days. Then she put aside her penitential garments and arrayed herself in her royal attire. Looking gorgeous, she approached the king, who sprang from the throne and welcomed her. What could he do for her, he asked.

Esther invited the king and Haman to a banquet. They accepted. During the banquet, Esther asked King Ahasuerus to spare her life and the lives of her people because an enemy was about to kill them.

"Who and where is the man who has dared to do this?" the king asked.

Esther replied, "The enemy oppressing us is this wicked Haman."

The king went into the garden in anger while Haman begged Esther for his life. When the king returned, he found that Haman had thrown himself on the couch with Esther. The king said, "Will he also violate the queen while she is with me in my own house?" He ordered that Haman be hung on the gibbet he had prepared for Mordecai.

The decree against the Jews was rescinded. Then the Jews took revenge by killing a great number of their enemies. Mordecai replaced Haman as second in command.

The Jews celebrate these events each year on the feast of Purim.

27

MOTHER AND SONS ARE MARTYRED

When we think of martyrs, we think first of Christians. But the Jews, too, had martyrs. An account of the martyrdom of a woman and her seven sons is in Chapter 7 of the Second Book of Maccabees.

It happened while the Greeks were occupying Palestine and insisting that the Jews obey Greek customs. King Antiochus IV forbade circumcision and the Jewish dietary laws. Those who disobeyed were tortured cruelly and put to death.

Nothing can be crueler than to force a mother to watch her sons be tortured and killed. That's what happened before Judas Maccabeus and his brothers rebelled against the Greeks in 165 B.C. And it was all over the refusal of her sons to eat pork.

The mother had clearly taught her sons to believe in the resurrection of the body, at least for the just. Belief in the resurrection was not part of Judaism from the beginning, but it's clear that it was taught by the time of the Maccabees.

I'll not go into the details of the torture of the seven brothers; you can look them up in your Bible if you're so inclined. For this book on biblical women, I'll concentrate on the actions of the mother.

The book praises her for encouraging her sons to die bravely. It says, "Most admirable and worthy of everlasting remembrance was the mother, who saw her seven sons perish in a single day, yet bore it courageously because of her hope in the Lord."

She spoke in Hebrew to her sons, telling them, "Since it is the Creator of the universe who shapes each man's beginning, as he brings about the origin of everything, he, in his mercy, will give you back both breath and life, because you now disregard yourselves for the sake of his law."

After six of the seven brothers had been killed, Antiochus appealed directly to the mother, urging her to advise her son to save his life. Finally, she went through the motions of persuading him. But again she spoke in Hebrew rather than Greek.

Leaning close to her son, she said, "Son, have pity on me, who carried you in my womb for nine months, nursed you for three years, brought you up, educated and supported you to your present age. I beg you, child, to look at the heavens and the earth and see all that is in them; then you will know that God did not make them out of existing things; and in the same way the human race came into existence. Do not be afraid of this executioner, but be worthy of your brothers and accept death, so that in the time of mercy I may receive you again with them."

Naturally, he proved to be as courageous as his brothers, telling the king that the king would not escape the hands of God. The king was enraged and treated him worse than the others before killing him.

The mother was the last to die.

PART II

WOMEN IN THE NEW TESTAMENT

28

ELIZABETH, WIFE OF ZECHARIAH

Chronologically, Elizabeth (her name means "worshiper of God") is the first woman named in the New Testament, in Chapter 1 of the Gospel According to Luke. She was the wife of Zechariah and the mother of St. John the Baptist.

In his account of the Annunciation, Luke has the angel Gabriel refer to Elizabeth as Mary's relative, nothing more specific. Earliest traditions say that she was a younger sister of Ann, Mary's mother, so she would have been Mary's aunt. Ann, though, doesn't appear in the Gospels so she technically was not a biblical woman. Her name comes from the early writing known as the *Protevangelium of James*, which tells of events that occurred before those in the Gospels.

Elizabeth and Zechariah lived in the hill country of Judea, in modern Ein Karem, a suburb of Jerusalem. Like some of the great women of the Old Testament (Sarah, Rebekah, Rachel, the mother of Samson, and Hannah), Elizabeth was childless and had reached menopause. Then the angel Gabriel appeared to Zechariah and told him that he and Elizabeth would have a child and that he should be called John.

Elizabeth did become pregnant shortly after that. As was customary, she went into seclusion, but she rejoiced that the Lord "has seen fit to take away my disgrace before others." Jews at the time considered barrenness as punishment for sin.

When Elizabeth was in the sixth month of her pregnancy, she had a surprise visit from her niece Mary. This scene, the Visitation, has been painted by many great artists.

Miraculous things occurred when Mary, pregnant with Jesus, greeted Elizabeth. First, as Elizabeth told her, "the infant in my womb leaped for joy" at the presence of Jesus. Some theologians have taught that this was a sign that John had been cleansed of original sin and would be born without original sin. (Only Jesus and Mary were *conceived* without original sin.) This fulfilled the promise made to Zechariah by Gabriel, who said about John, "He will be filled with the Holy Spirit even from his mother's womb." If he was filled with the Holy Spirit he would no longer have original sin.

Then Elizabeth herself was cleansed from original sin since Luke says that she, too, was filled with the Holy Spirit. She cried out to Mary, "Most blessed are you among women and blessed is the fruit of your womb," words that would become part of the Hail Mary.

Mary stayed with Elizabeth for three months, so it's assumed that she was there to assist at John's birth. It would be strange for her to stay with Elizabeth up to the time the birth was imminent and then leave.

Eight days after the baby's birth, friends and neighbors gathered for his circumcision. They were surprised when Elizabeth announced that his name would be John. They even argued with her, pointing out that no one in the family had that name. Zechariah, who had been unable to speak since Gabriel appeared to him, settled the matter when he wrote on a tablet, "His name is John."

We know nothing more about Elizabeth and Zechariah.

29

MARY, THE MOTHER OF GOD

Mary, the mother of Jesus, is the greatest of all the biblical women. It's more than fitting, therefore, that there is more about her in the Bible than any of the other women.

Although there are legends about Mary's birth and childhood in the *Protevangelium of James*, we first meet her in the Gospels when she is a teenager living in Nazareth. She was betrothed to Joseph; that is, they were married but had not yet had the celebration at which Joseph would take her to his home. Marriage for the Jews at that time consisted of two parts. The first was the betrothal, the consent of both parties in the presence of at least two competent witnesses, the actual wedding. But they continued to live apart while a celebration was being planned for the solemn entry of the bride into the groom's home some months later.

One day the angel Gabriel appeared to Mary and told her that, of all the women in the world, she had been chosen to be the mother of the Son of the Most High. Mary was curious, though, to know how that could be since she had taken a vow of chastity. Joseph, believed to be older, apparently agreed not to have sexual relations with her.

Gabriel replied that Mary would remain a virgin because the Holy Spirit would come upon her and her son would be the Son of God. Obviously, therefore, she would be the mother of God. She must have been satisfied with this explanation because she accepted: "Behold, I am the handmaid of the Lord. May it be done to me according to your word." With her *fiat*, she became pregnant.

The angel had also told her that her relative Elizabeth (believed to be her aunt; see previous chapter) was also pregnant. Mary trusted the angel's word and immediately set out to visit her. How did she tell Joseph that she had to take a trip to Judea, a trip of five to seven days, and that she would be gone three months? Did she, a teenage girl, travel alone in one of the caravans that made the trip? Luke doesn't tell us, but it's pretty apparent that Mary was a very self-sufficient young woman.

When she arrived at Elizabeth's home, Elizabeth was inspired by the Holy Spirit to praise Mary: "Most blessed are you among women, and blessed is the fruit of your womb." She recognized Mary as "the mother of my Lord." Then Luke inserts Mary's Magnificat, a hymn of praise that might have been a Jewish Christian hymn. In it, Mary says, "From now on all ages will call me blessed."

Mary presumably remained with Elizabeth

until Elizabeth's son, who would become John the Baptist, was born, and then returned to Nazareth. It was probably at this time that Joseph learned that Mary was pregnant. How could he not believe that she had been unfaithful to him? He knew that he wasn't the father, so what other explanation could there be? He decided to divorce her quietly.

Then, in a dream, Joseph learned that there was indeed another explanation. An angel appeared and told him that "it is through the Holy Spirit that this child has been conceived in her." That was enough for Joseph, who took Mary into his home.

Jesus was born in Bethlehem, a town in Judea, so Joseph and Mary again had to make a week-long journey similar to that which Mary took when she visited Elizabeth—from Nazareth to the Sea of Galilee, down the east side of the Jordan River to Jericho to avoid traveling through Samaria, and then up to Jerusalem and Bethlehem.

As we all know, Bethlehem was crowded and Joseph and Mary found shelter in a cave, where Jesus was born. I need not go into the details of the visit of the shepherds, and later the Magi from the east. Both groups were inspired to recognize that God had come into the world. "And Mary kept all these things, reflecting on them in her heart."

Mary is present next during Jesus' presentation in the Temple when he was forty days old. She and Joseph were following the Mosaic Law that required a woman who had had a son to be purified forty days after the birth. Until then she was forbidden to touch anything sacred or to enter the Temple area.

During this visit, Simeon was inspired by God to recognize Jesus as the long-awaited Messiah. But he also warned Mary that she, too, would suffer—"you yourself a sword will pierce." The Church considers this as the first of Mary's seven sorrows.

Although Luke tells us that the Holy Family returned to Nazareth, Matthew's Gospel tells us about their flight to Egypt to escape the wrath of King Herod. This is the second of Mary's seven sorrows. Matthew says that they remained in Egypt until after Herod's death, when they returned and settled in Nazareth.

There's nothing more about the family until Jesus was twelve years old, although Luke says that each year they made the long trip to Jerusalem for the feast of Passover. Mary and Joseph were raising Jesus in the traditions of Israel, as a faithful Jewish boy.

When Jesus was twelve, though, he stayed in Jerusalem when his parents joined the caravan for the return trip. We can imagine Mary and Joseph thinking that he was with his friends. What twelve-year-old would stay with his parents? When they realized that he was not in the caravan, they returned to Jerusalem, where they found Jesus in the Temple in the midst of the teachers. This loss of the Child Jesus was the third of Mary's sorrows. The last four involve her son's passion and death: his carrying his cross to Calvary, his crucifixion, his being taken down from the cross and laid in her arms, and his burial.

Mary's first appearance in the Bible after Jesus has grown is at Cana, where Jesus performed his first public miracle by changing water into wine. By this time Joseph apparently has died and Mary would have been in her mid-forties. She and Jesus had been invited to a wedding—apparently a large celebration since Mary noticed that the host had run out of wine. When she tells Jesus about this, you get the impression that Jesus must have performed miracles at home because Mary is confident that he can do something. She simply tells the servers, "Do whatever he tells you," the last words she speaks in the Bible. Then, as we know, Jesus did what Mary expected.

After the wedding celebration, Mary accompanied Jesus to Capernaum, where Jesus was then living with his new disciple Peter.

We don't know how often, if at all, Mary was with Jesus during his public life. There is the incident when Jesus was told that his mother and brothers had come to see him. He used the occasion to say that "whoever does the will of God is my brother and sister and mother." Presumably, he got together with his family later.

Mary was in Jerusalem during the last days of Jesus' life, probably because she maintained the tradition of going there for Passover. It's a bit strange that only John's Gospel places Mary at the foot of the cross. That Gospel tells us that Jesus entrusted his mother to John while hanging on the cross.

The Gospels don't tell us that Jesus appeared to his mother after his resurrection, but how can we imagine that he did not? We know that Mary was still with Jesus' followers in Jerusalem after his resurrection and ascension because the Acts of the Apostles says that the small community included "some women, and Mary the mother of Jesus, and his brothers." She apparently was there on the day of Pentecost, when the Holy Spirit descended upon the Apostles.

Then Mary disappears from the Bible. What we believe about her after Pentecost comes from tradition and speculation. She probably continued to live in Jerusalem with John or James—not John's brother but the James identified as the brother of Jesus who became the leader of the Church in Jerusalem.

Tradition says that Mary died at age seventy, probably in Jerusalem where the Church of the Dormition is today. The Tomb of Mary is located next to the Garden of Gethsemane. It's believed that Mary was buried there and from there was assumed into heaven.

But there's also a tradition that Mary went

with John to Ephesus in Turkey and died there. I favor Jerusalem. If John went to Ephesus I think it was after Mary's death, which probably was around the year 50. She would have died before Paul lived in Ephesus and well before Paul wrote his letters to the Ephesians.

30

THE WOMAN AT THE WELL

The fourth chapter of John's Gospel tells us about Jesus' meeting with a Samaritan woman at Jacob's well in Samaria. John calls the town Sychar but St. Jerome identified it as Schechem, the capital of the Kingdom of Israel and, later, Samaria. It's modern Nablus and Jacob's well is still there. I visited it before pilgrims stopped going there because of the Israeli-Palestinian conflict.

Jesus was traveling from Judea back to Galilee. Normally Jews would take a route across the Jordan River to avoid walking through Samaria, but Jesus decided to take the more direct, but more mountainous, route. His disciples went into town to buy food while Jesus sat by the well.

At noon a Samaritan woman came to get water and Jesus asked her for a drink of water. This was surprising, to say the least, since Jews never used anything in common with Samaritans, especially Samaritan women whom they regarded as ritually impure.

The animosity between Jews and Samaritans went all the way back to the years after Assyria conquered the Kingdom of Israel in 722 B.C. Thousands of Jews were deported to Assyria and people from ten other nations were allowed to fill the void in Israel. The Jews who remained in Israel, now called Samaria, intermarried with the newcomers, resulting in a mixed race with a mixed religion. After the Jews who later were exiled to Babylon after the fall of the Kingdom of Judah returned, they refused to accept the Samaritans.

The woman at the well wasn't the most savory of women. She had had five husbands and was then living with another man. Nevertheless, she engaged Jesus in a conversation about the differences in belief between the Jews and Samaritans. She said that her ancestors worshiped on Mount Gerizim in Samaria (in a temple they built in the fourth century B.C.) while the Jews worshiped in Jerusalem. Jesus replied that, although salvation is *from* the Jews, it is not only *for* the Jews, but for all who adore God.

The most startling part of the conversation happened when the woman said that she knew that the Messiah was coming. Jesus replied, "I am he," which could also be translated "I am," God's name in the Old Testament. This was the first time he had acknowledged to anyone that he was the Messiah.

When Jesus' disciples returned with food,

they were shocked to find him talking with a Samaritan woman. While Jesus talked with the disciples, the woman quickly ran into the city and told her neighbors, "Come see a man who told me everything I have done [a bit of an exaggeration]. Could he possibly be the Messiah?" A footnote in John's Gospel says that the woman is thus presented as a missionary.

Some of the people returned to the well with the woman and asked Jesus to remain with them, which he did for two days. Thus did Jesus make his first non-Jewish converts as a result of his meeting with the woman at the well.

31

HERODIAS AND SALOME

Herodias and Salome, her daughter, appear in the fourteenth chapter of Matthew's Gospel and the sixth chapter of Mark's. The daughter's name is not mentioned in either account, but Salome has become her traditional name.

Mark's account says that Herodias was married to Herod Antipas, the ruler of Galilee and Perea. Perea was east of the Jordan River in what is now Jordan. When King Herod the Great died in 4 B.C. his territory was divided among three of his surviving sons (he had had three other sons executed): Archelaus received Judea; Herod Antipas, Galilee and Perea; and Philip, the land north and east of the Sea of Galilee in what is now the Golan Heights. In 6 A.D., the Romans took over Judea from Archelaus.

According to both Gospels, Herodias (Herod the Great's granddaughter) previously had been married to Philip. It was undoubtedly a great scandal when she left Philip for his half-brother,

Herod Antipas. At least the matter was sufficiently notorious that John the Baptist told Herod, "It is not lawful for you to have your brother's wife." John quoted Leviticus 18:16: "You shall not have intercourse with your brother's wife, for that would be a disgrace to your brother."

The impertinence of this man angered Herodias. At her insistence, Herod had John thrown into prison. But that didn't satisfy Herodias; she wanted John put to death, to get rid of him entirely. Herod hesitated. He feared the people, who regarded John as a prophet. Besides, he was strangely attracted to him, regarded him as a holy man, and enjoyed listening to him.

Then came Herodias's chance. Herod had a large birthday party, and the wine flowed freely. As part of the entertainment, Salome (Herod's niece and Philip's daughter) came in and danced. The dance has been called elsewhere the dance of seven veils, but not in the Gospels. We can imagine, though, that it was sensuous and erotic. Herod was so pleased that he told Salome she could have anything she wanted, "even half of my kingdom."

Hurrying to her mother, Salome asked, "What shall I ask for?"

Herodias didn't hesitate, "The head of John the Baptist."

Salome returned to Herod. "I want you to give me at once on a platter the head of John the Baptist," she said.

King Herod sobered up quickly. He didn't want that but, since his guests had heard what he had said, he quickly sent an executioner to the prison with orders to behead John and bring back his head. And so it was done. John's head was brought back on a platter and given to Salome, who in turn gave it to her mother.

Herod Antipas and Herodias ruled until the year 41. At that time, Emperor Caligula made Herodias's brother, Herod Agrippa, King of the Jews. Antipas and Herodias went to Rome to get Caligula to reverse his decision, but he would not. Instead, Antipas and Herodias were sent into exile. We don't know what happened to Salome.

32

STORIES OF TWO PUBLIC SINNERS

The Gospels have two stories about Jesus' relations with women who were public sinners.

The first is in the seventh chapter of Luke's Gospel. While Jesus was dining in the home of a Pharisee, reclining on his side with his feet behind him in the normal posture of guests at a banquet in those days, a disreputable woman suddenly appeared behind him. We know nothing about her except that she was a sinful woman (she was not Mary Magdalene), but she presumably had heard Jesus teaching in the city and felt an overwhelming sorrow for her sins.

She stood behind Jesus, crying bitterly, so copiously that she could bathe Jesus' feet with her tears and then wipe them with her long hair. Then she kissed Jesus' feet and anointed them with ointment that she had brought in an alabaster flask.

The self-righteous Pharisee thought to himself, "If this man were a prophet, he would know who and what sort of woman this is who is touching him, that she is a sinner."

Of course, Jesus did know what sort of woman she was. He told the Pharisee, "Her many sins have been forgiven; hence, she has shown great love."

Then he told the woman, "Your sins are forgiven. Your faith has saved you; go in peace."

Others at the table said to themselves, "Who is this who even forgives sins?" However, Jesus really said that she was forgiven because of her sorrow and her faith. That the woman's sins had been forgiven was then attested by the great love she showed toward Jesus.

The second story is now at the beginning of the eighth chapter of John's Gospel, but it wasn't always there. It has been in different places in different manuscripts and the language and style is more Luke's than John's. Nevertheless, it is canonical Scripture.

It's the story of the woman caught in adultery. Scribes and Pharisees brought her to Jesus in the Temple area in Jerusalem. They wanted to test Jesus to bring a charge against him. They told him that Moses commanded them to stone women caught in adultery, but asked what he said. (Actually, Leviticus 20:10 and Deuteronomy 22:22 say that both the man and the woman who commit adultery should be put to death, but don't say anything about stoning.)

We know the rest of the story, of course. Jesus bent over and wrote in the dust for awhile. Finally he stood up and said, "Let the one among you who is without sin be the first to throw a stone at her." The scribes and Pharisees, one by one, walked away, leaving Jesus alone with the woman.

Jesus said, "Where are they? Has no one condemned you?" When the woman replied no, Jesus said, "Neither do I condemn you. Go, and from now on do not sin any more." He obviously didn't condone the sin of adultery since he told her not to sin any more, but he also refused to judge her.

33

MARY MAGDALENE

Mary Magdalene has fascinated writers, and artists, for nearly two millennia. More probably has been written about her than about any other biblical woman except the Blessed Virgin. In recent years she has been called Jesus' lover and the mother of his children (or at least child). Through the centuries she has been identified as one, or both, of the public sinners in the previous chapter. She has also been confused with Mary of Bethany, sister of Martha and Lazarus. A shrine in the village of St. Maximin la Sainte Baume, France claims that Mary Magdalene lived and died there with her brother Lazarus and sister Martha.

None of this is in the New Testament. What we know from the Bible is that Mary was from Magdala, a large fishing village on the Sea of Galilee. She became the leader of the women followers of Jesus who traveled with him and the Apostles and supported them out of their resources, just as Peter was the leader of the men.

We also know that "seven demons had gone out" of Mary, but we don't know what that means. That phrase in Luke 8:2 is undoubtedly what prompted some people, including Pope Gregory the Great, to assume that Mary was a repentant sinner, but it's more likely that she had suffered from illness of some kind.

We also know from the Bible that Mary was present at Jesus' crucifixion, was one of the women who went to the tomb with spices and perfumed oil on the Sunday after the crucifixion, and was the first person to whom Jesus appeared after his resurrection.

That's what we know about Mary Magdalene from the Bible, and it should be enough to realize what a special person she was. Everything else written about her is either speculation or comes from early documents written by people with specific agendas.

There's an apocryphal Gospel of Mary Magdalene, for example, that claims that Jesus wanted Mary, not Peter, to be head of his Church. This supposedly was suppressed by the male hierarchy. The writing shows hostility toward Mary on the part of Peter. We can speculate that perhaps Peter and Mary didn't always get along—after all, the Gospels show that there were arguments among the Apostles—but it doesn't seem likely that Jesus wanted Mary to head his Church.

What role did Mary play in the early Church?

We can speculate all we want, but the fact is that we don't know. As the leader of the women who followed Jesus, and as close to him as she obviously was since he chose her to appear to first, we would expect her to have played an active role indeed. We would assume that she was present at Pentecost when the Holy Spirit descended on those in the Upper Room, but Luke doesn't specifically mention her in the Acts of the Apostles.

Can't we be satisfied in knowing that Mary Magdalene was Jesus' favorite among his women followers?

34

MARTHA AND MARY OF BETHANY

Martha and Mary were sisters who lived in Bethany, about two miles from the top of the Mount of Olives where a road led down to Jerusalem. They had a brother named Lazarus. We don't know how the three siblings met Jesus, but he became a good friend who, apparently, frequently stayed with them when he was in Jerusalem, although the Gospels don't specifically say that. Matthew's Gospel says that Jesus left Jerusalem after his procession into the city and spent the night in Bethany, and we have come to assume that he went to their home.

We first meet Martha and Mary in Luke's Gospel, the end of Chapter 10. In this episode, Martha was busy getting the meal ready while Mary sat at Jesus' feet listening to him speak. This tells us something about Jesus' attitude toward women since, in first-century Palestine, it would have been remarkable for a woman to assume the position of a disciple. It also tells us that Jesus felt relaxed in their home.

In this episode, Martha asked Jesus to tell Mary to help her serve dinner, but Jesus replied that Mary "has chosen the better part and it will not be taken from her." We get the idea that Mary was more contemplative while Martha was more active. Perhaps, though, Jesus wanted to make the point that a hostess shouldn't get so involved with preparing the meal that she neglects her guests.

Strangely, Luke doesn't mention the sisters' brother Lazarus. We learn about him in John's Gospel, which also is the one that tells us that they lived in Bethany. This was the story about Jesus raising Lazarus from the dead. When Lazarus became ill, the sisters sent word to Jesus, "Master, the one you love is ill," telling us that Jesus had developed a close relationship with him.

In his book *Jesus: A Meditation on His Stories and His Relationships With Women*, Father Andrew Greeley expresses his opinion that Martha and Mary were teenagers and that Lazarus was even younger, twelve or thirteen. I cannot agree. First of all, John's Gospel says, "A *man* was ill, Lazarus from Bethany." It hardly seems probable that Jesus would have developed such a close relationship with a boy. I have always imagined Lazarus as about Jesus' age, with Martha and Mary in their twenties. If they were only teenagers or younger, who was the head of the household?

In the story of the raising of Lazarus, Martha first ran to meet Jesus and expressed her belief in the resurrection of the body and in Jesus as the Messiah. Mary, too, hurried to meet him when she learned that he had arrived.

Martha, Mary and Lazarus were also present at another meal in Bethany before Jesus' crucifixion. This time, John says, Mary took a liter of perfumed oil and anointed Jesus' feet with it. (Matthew and Mark say that she poured it on his head.)

This is the last time they appear in the Scriptures. Accounts of their later lives are only speculation.

35

FOUR WHOM JESUS HEALED

The Gospels tell us about four instances in which Jesus healed women—or girls in two cases.

The first occurred when Jesus was in Capernaum. A synagogue official there named Jairus asked Jesus to come to his home and cure his twelve-year-old daughter. Recognizing the official's faith, Jesus started to go off with him, followed by a large crowd.

But before they got to Jairus's home, we get the story of a woman who had been afflicted with hemorrhages for twelve years. The first-century doctors couldn't seem to help her. A woman who was menstruating was considered to be ritually unclean and was not supposed to have physical contact with others. But this woman was desperate. She hoped that perhaps she would be healed if she could only touch part of his clothing—the tassel on his cloak, according to Matthew's account. (The Mosaic Law prescribed that tassels be worn on the corners of one's garment as a reminder to keep the Commandments.)

When she did touch Jesus' clothing, her flow of blood immediately dried up. But Jesus somehow realized that power had gone out of him, looked around and asked, "Who touched my clothes?" The woman approached and told him the whole story. Jesus told her that her faith had saved her and bade her go in peace.

With the woman cured, he continued toward Jairus's house. They were met by people who informed them that Jairus's daughter had died. Jesus ignored them and told Jairus, "Don't be afraid; just have faith." Earlier Jairus had faith that Jesus could heal his daughter, so Jesus told him to just continue to have faith.

When Jesus told the crowd at the home that the girl was only sleeping, they ridiculed him. He took Jairus and his wife to the girl's bedside and told the girl to get up. She did so immediately, and began to walk around.

A third healing also involved a girl. This time it happened in the district of Tyre, in modern Lebanon. A Canaanite woman, not a Jew, approached Jesus and begged him to drive a demon out of her daughter. At first Jesus demurred, saying that he was sent only to the lost sheep of the house of Israel. He even seemed insulting when he said, "It is not right to take the food of the children and throw it to the dogs."

The woman, though, was persistent. "Please, Lord," she said, "for even the dogs eat the scraps that fall from the table of their masters." That did the trick. Jesus recognized how great the woman's faith was and told her that her daughter was healed. She was.

The fourth healing was of an elderly woman who appeared to be suffering from osteoporosis because, Luke says, "she was bent over, completely incapable of standing erect." She had been that way for eighteen years. Jesus laid hands on her and she at once stood up straight. This time it didn't seem to depend on the woman's faith.

36

WITNESSES TO THE CRUCIFIXION

Who were some of the women mentioned by name who were present when Jesus was crucified, besides Jesus' mother Mary and Mary Magdalene? And who were those who went to the tomb on the following Sunday, planning to anoint Jesus' body?

We know, first of all, from Luke's Gospel, that those named were among the women from Galilee who traveled with Jesus and the Apostles and supported them out of their resources. Susanna was named by Luke as one of the women, but she is not specifically named at the crucifixion, so she might or might not have been there.

Matthew's Gospel names Mary the mother of James (one of the Apostles) and Joseph, whom he also calls "the other Mary." She is sometimes identified as the wife of Clopas, who might have been Joseph's brother and, therefore, the Blessed Virgin's brother-in-law. However, the Apostle James is also identified as the son of Alphaeus, so this Mary might have been his wife. Matthew's

Gospel says that she went with Mary Magdalene to the tomb on Easter. They were told by an angel that Jesus had risen, went to tell the Apostles, and were met by Jesus on the way.

Mark's Gospel adds Salome, the wife of Zebedee and mother of the Apostles James and John, both at the crucifixion and at the tomb. We met Salome earlier, in Matthew's Gospel, when she approached Jesus with her sons and asked him to "command that these two sons of mine sit, one at your right and the other at your left, in your kingdom." (Mark's Gospel says that the two Apostles themselves asked. We don't know why Matthew, who got the story from Mark, added Salome.)

Luke's Gospel doesn't mention any of the women present at the crucifixion by name, saying only, "The women who had come from Galilee with him followed behind [while Jesus was being buried], and when they had seen the tomb and the way in which his body was laid in it, they returned and prepared spices and perfumed oils."

However, Luke does identify those women when they went to the tomb on Sunday: Mary Magdalene, Joanna, and Mary the mother of James. It's the only mention of Joanna during the crucifixion, but Luke earlier identified her as the wife of King Herod's steward, Chuza. We don't know anything else about her, but it's interesting that one of Jesus' close followers was connected to Herod Antipas.

All of these women probably were among those who remained with the Apostles in Jerusalem after Jesus' ascension and were present when the Holy Spirit descended upon them on Pentecost.

Before I finish writing about the women in the Gospels and move on to the Acts of the Apostles, I should mention Peter's mother-in-law. She appears very briefly, two verses in Matthew's Gospel and three in Mark's. In Capernaum, Jesus went to the house of Peter and his brother Andrew, where Peter's mother-in-law was ill. Jesus cured her so she could get up and wait on them (Matthew says "him"). It's probably best that I not say any more about that.

37

SAPPHIRA, TABITHA AND LYDIA

Don't lie to St. Peter! According to Chapter 5 of the Acts of the Apostles, Sapphira did, and look what happened to her.

The early Church held everything in common, much like a religious order today. Acts says that those who owned property or houses would sell them and lay the proceeds of the sale at the feet of the Apostles. Then the proceeds were distributed to each according to need.

Sapphira and her husband Ananias decided not to do that. After they sold a piece of property, they kept some of the proceeds for themselves. Ananias, who wasn't with Sapphira at the time, put the remainder at the feet of the Apostles.

Peter wasn't dumb. He said to Ananias, "Why has Satan filled your heart so that you lied to the Holy Spirit and retained part of the price of the land?… You have lied not to human beings, but to God." When Ananias heard those words, he fell down dead. Men came in, carried him out and buried him.

Three hours later Sapphira came in, unaware of what had happened. Peter said to her, "Tell me, did you sell the land for this amount?"

"Yes, for that amount," she answered.

"Listen," Peter said, "the footsteps of those who have buried your husband are at the door, and they will carry you out." Sapphira too fell down dead. They buried her next to her husband.

Another woman, though, expressed the right attitude toward material possessions. Her name was Tabitha in Aramaic, or Dorcas in Greek (both words meant "gazelle"). Chapter 9 of Acts says that she lived in Joppa (near modern Tel Aviv). She was completely occupied with good deeds and alms-giving, particularly known for the tunics and cloaks she made for others. But she fell sick and died.

Peter was in Lydda, near Joppa, at the time, so two men went to tell him about Tabitha's death. Peter went to Joppa and was taken to an upstairs room where widows were weeping. Peter sent them out of the room, knelt by Tabitha and prayed, and then said, "Tabitha, rise up."

She opened her eyes, saw Peter, and sat up. Peter helped her to her feet and took her to the mourning widows. Naturally, this miracle became widely known throughout Joppa, resulting in numerous conversions. Peter then remained in Joppa for a long time, with a man named Simon, a tanner.

Lydia was another woman in Acts, Chapter 16. Paul met her when he went to Philippi, in Macedonia. One day he went along a river where women had gathered, probably doing their laundry. Lydia, described as "a dealer in purple cloth, from the city of Thyatira, a worshiper of God," was among them. After listening to Paul, she and her household were baptized. Then she invited Paul to stay at her home, and Paul did so.

Later, after Paul and Silas were released from prison in Philippi, they returned to Lydia's home, where Christians were assembled.

38

MARK'S MOTHER AND RHODA

Poor Rhoda. When this incident happened, she never expected that we'd be reading about it almost two thousand years later. I guess Luke thought it was so funny that he couldn't resist inserting it when he wrote his Acts of the Apostles. It's a change from most of Acts, which is all so serious.

In fact, the chapter that reports the incident, Chapter 12, couldn't be much more serious because it begins with King Herod Agrippa executing the Apostle James. Then he arrested Peter and put him in prison under the guard of four squads of four soldiers each. He obviously was determined that Peter wouldn't escape.

But he did. While he was sleeping between two soldiers an angel tapped him on his side and told him to get up. The chains fell from his wrists. The angel told him to put on his cloak, belt and sandals and to follow him. They passed the first guard, then the second, and came to an iron gate leading out to the city, which opened by itself. After they emerged and were walking down an alley, the angel left him.

All this time Peter had thought he was having a dream, but he finally recovered his senses and realized that the angel had rescued him. He made his way to the home of Mary, the mother of a disciple named John but who was called Mark. Many of Peter's friends and followers were assembled there in prayer. Mary's home seems to have been the gathering place for the Christians in Jerusalem.

Rhoda was a maid in Mary's home. Peter knocked on the gateway door, and Rhoda answered it. She asked who was there. When she recognized Peter's voice, instead of opening the door, she ran to tell the others that Peter was at the gate. They told her that she must be out of her mind, but she insisted that Peter was there.

Meanwhile, poor Peter was left standing at the door, still knocking to get in. Finally, someone had the sense to open the door and let him in. He quietly explained what had happened to him and told those present to report it to James, the leader of the Church in Jerusalem, and to the other Apostles. Then, hoping not to endanger those present, he left and went someplace else.

When Herod Agrippa discovered the next day that Peter had escaped, he ordered the guards to be tried and executed.

Mary's son John, who was called Mark, later accompanied Paul and Barnabas on their first missionary journey, but deserted them. When they were planning their second trip, Barnabas wanted to take John Mark again, but Paul refused to take him. So Paul and Barnabas separated, Barnabas taking Mark to Cyprus.

In Jerusalem today, St. Mark's Syrian Orthodox Church is built on the site of John Mark's mother's home. When I was there in 1997 during the Week of Prayer for Christian Unity, one of our prayer services was held there.

39

PRISCA, PAUL'S COLLABORATOR

I conclude this book about biblical women with Priscilla, as she is called in the Acts of the Apostles, or Prisca as St. Paul called her more familiarly in his letters. Other women are named in some of Paul's letters, but we don't know much about them.

Prisca was Paul's closest female collaborator. He first met her and her husband Aquila when he went to Corinth, Greece. Prisca and Aquila weren't Paul's converts though. They had already become Christians in Rome, but we don't know when or how. We do know, though, that they left Rome in the year 41 when Emperor Claudius expelled the Jews from Rome because of disturbances among the Jews "at the instigation of Chrestos," according to the Roman historian Suetonius. This apparently meant disagreement over the Messiahship of Jesus.

Like Paul, Prisca and Aquila were tentmakers. When Paul arrived in Corinth, he went job hunting. Prisca and Aquila hired him. Imagine their surprise when Paul began to preach about Jesus and they realized that they had the same beliefs. Prisca and Aquila's home soon became a gathering place for the Christians Paul converted.

Paul remained in Corinth for eighteen months before moving on. He took Prisca and Aquila with him to Ephesus and left them there to establish a Christian community while he continued on to Macedonia. Paul was expecting a lot, since Prisca and Aquila had to abandon the business they had in Corinth and start anew in Ephesus. But when Paul returned to Ephesus a year later, he found a thriving church.

While Paul was gone, Apollos arrived in Ephesus. He was a Jew from Alexandria who had learned about Jesus. He preached about him in the synagogue, but he knew only about the baptism of John. Prisca and Aquila took him aside and explained things more accurately. When Apollos decided he wanted to go to Corinth, they wrote letters to their friends there to welcome him.

Prisca and Aquila were doing fine in Ephesus, but Paul decided to uproot them again. This time he wanted them to return to Rome as his advance team, to make Paul known to the Roman Christians before Paul went there. This was the year 54, a full thirteen years since Claudius had expelled the Jews, so it was safe for them to return. They probably were happy to be returning home.

Paul was planning to write a letter to the

Romans before he went to Rome, and he wanted it to be a personal letter. He asked Prisca and Aquila to give him the names of some of the leading Christians so he could include them in the letter. They did and Paul's letter mentions twenty-four individuals by name.

Of course, Paul didn't get to Rome until much later than he expected, probably the year 60. Before going to Rome he took a collection to Jerusalem where he was arrested and spent three years in prison.

We don't know what happened to Prisca and Aquila after Paul's execution.